# Surviving

## the

# Aftermath

## of

# Suicide

## A Daughter's Journey

## Jennifer Boutilier

**Disclaimer**

The author wishes to acknowledge that this book was written strictly from her perspective only as part of her own personal journey in dealing with her mother's loss. Accounts and events depicted may not (and cannot) reflect the perspective or viewpoints of others. The author understands and accepts the fact that there were other extenuating issues and circumstances leading to her mother's death that others would have been privy to, but she has chosen to write of only those she was aware of that affected her personally. Names have been changed to maintain anonymity.

# Dedication

---

This book is dedicated to my mom

who always saw the good things in my life

and told me that I could do anything

I set my mind to.

# Table of Contents

# Acknowledgements

I would personally like to thank two very important sources of support and encouragement that assisted me during this entire process: first, Kathleen Mailer, who kept me accountable to how I was doing on my book and allowed me to talk while she listened. She acted as a sounding board for all the ideas of what I wanted to include within these pages. She let me know if she agreed with an idea or not and was instrumental in helping this book come to fruition.

Second, my Word of Life church family. There are so many people that I could include in this, but I think you know who you are. You are the ones who kept me sane the entire time I wanted to give up on my church life after I found out that my mom was gone.

You helped me stay grounded and, when I told you that I was writing this book about dealing with the aftermath of suicide, you encouraged me all the way to the end.

# Forward

By John Mainer

I have known Jennifer since she was born and I knew her mom Kathy, for a long time before that. I first met Kathy when she was a young teenager, in Sea Cadets, in Winnipeg. I was a Sea Cadet Officer at that time and had the opportunity to teach Kathy for several years within the organization. I didn't know Kathy outside of cadets at first. However, as time progressed she, like many other sea cadets upon finishing their time as a cadet by 'aging out', became a cadet officer like myself. A few years later, Kathy and her soon-to-be husband, also within the cadet organization, announced their engagement. They began a life together, seemingly happy at the time - buying a home and starting a family.

Slowly, I began to know a different Kathy; a more mature young woman, a mom, a wife, an officer, a worker - yes, but one who developed or perpetuated some mental health issues. Some of the signs were noticeable and manageable, others not so much. Some of the un-manageable issues caused strife for her young family, especially for her husband and for Jennifer, who was the eldest of three siblings.

Her husband, after dealing for some time with the issues the family had to face, decided a separation from Kathy and her emotional difficulties was warranted. It was those same un-noticed or un-manageable issues that would later in her life, allow the demons to take over and demand Kathy take leave of the life she had. They were unexplainable reasons to those of us who do not understand the demons, or what causes of them to exist.

I, along with many others, was shocked and saddened deeply to learn of Kathy's life-ending decision. I remember I cried alongside friends, associates and family members. Jennifer asked me to speak at her mom's service, to which I was proud to do so.

The 'journey' of which Jennifer has written of, is amazing. For those of us not directly associated, or impacted with the struggles one faces with a family member living with the demons, it is hard to imagine what Jennifer has had to endure, before and after her mom's suicide. Knowing what I know and being able to put faces, places and dates to the words that she writes, I found myself on a couple of occasions openly weeping for her while reading her book. I think the book is amazingly well written for one with no experience in writing, other than personal journals and diaries of which most young girls partake at one time or another. I am very proud of Jennifer, both as my friend's daughter and as my 'niece'. We are not related by blood, but that makes no difference to me and I am just as certain it doesn't for her, either.

I am, and will always be, Uncle John to Jennifer and I am proud to say so. Well done, young lady, or as your mom may have said in such a circumstance – bravo zulu!

# Introduction:

---

# WHEN SUICIDE ROCKS

# YOUR WORLD

Shock... horror.... disbelief! If you have ever lost someone very special to you to suicide, you know these emotions first-hand; you have felt them tear through your very being, leaving you in a state of utter devastation and despair. Trust me. I know. I've been there. I know exactly what thoughts start racing through your head; questions like, "Why did they do it?", "What could I have done to prevent it?" and, "How can I possibly keep going on with life?"

In the year 2009, I experienced the loss of my mother to suicide. The pain I felt was indescribable, as was the sense of loss and confusion. I didn't know what to believe, or where to turn. I searched desperately for answers to the swarms of questions I struggled with, but there wasn't much of anything that offered solace, or solutions. It was in that search that I realized, if I was struggling with these questions, others probably were, too. And if my experience was true to form, others were going to continue to struggle with them long into the future.

I never, in my wildest dreams (or nightmares in this case), imagined that suicide would ever rock my world in the manner that it did! The tragedy of someone taking their own life was always something that happened 'out there', off in the distance; not up close and personal, and certainly not so close to home as your own mother!

Surviving the aftermath of suicide is torturous and painful for those left behind. Days of agonizing sorrow turn to weeks of heartache. Weeks of heartache stretch into months of confusion and unanswered questions; the months of confusion meld into years of soul-searching and, inevitably, self-discovery.

Throughout the process, there were people, tools and coping strategies that I desperately depended on and utilized that played key roles in surviving the aftermath of my mother's suicide. I pass these tools and strategies on in the hopes that they will offer support and encouragement to you and to others who have experienced the devastating suicide of a loved one.

I want you to know that there is hope and there is light at the end of this seemingly endless tunnel! It does get easier, even though you might not think so right now. Even as I am writing this, thinking about the pain, it is much easier to talk about now than it was when it happened. The times where I just wanted to cry and didn't want to believe that my mother was gone, have diminished. Time, as they say, does heal. The emotional pain gradually dissipates and makes facing the future more manageable.

Truth is, if we stay in the stage of pain and desolation; in that state where we just want to give up, we wouldn't get anywhere in life. The grieving time for everyone is so different and I know these words don't help much when you feel like the world is crashing in around you. But, I want to reassure you that I do understand; I am with you and I am holding you in prayer as you go through this process of dealing with your loss.

In the event that you were the one who found your loved one, I can only imagine your pain. I was not the one who discovered my mom that fateful day and I, truthfully, cannot give any answers as to the shock and horror you must have experienced upon finding someone you love killed by their own hand. But I pray that you might find some nugget of truth and support in the pages of this book; that you might find some comfort in the words of one who has also searched for answers. Don't give up! There is hope. There is always hope!

*"Do not be afraid for I am with you. Do not be discouraged for I am Your God. I will strengthen you and help you. I will hold you up with my victorious right hand."*

Isaiah 41:10 NLT

# Chapter 1:

## PRAY FOR STRENGTH

Prayer: I am convinced that prayer is the answer to everything and anything we need; especially in situations such as the one I found myself in. One straightforward, effective prayer anyone can use in any situation is simply, "God, help!"

I remember the day my life changed forever. I had no idea what had happened, when my dad called me asking what I was doing and where I was. Since my dad doesn't normally just call me and start asking questions like that, I immediately became suspicious. But all he would tell me was that I needed to call him when I got home. He sounded very serious and I could sense something was very wrong.

To help keep my thoughts straight and positive, I prayed. I prayed for strength and I prayed for understanding of whatever was going on. I sent out a text to about twenty friends, including a couple of pastors, asking them to do the same. I explained that I didn't know what was going on, but I was worried. They all responded with, "We will be praying."

My boyfriend was expecting me to call him when I got off work and when I did, I poured everything out; the fact that my dad had called me asking me where I was and what I was doing, that his voice had sounded so very ominous and that I was really scared. I really just needed someone to talk to, to release my emotions and get my thoughts in line. I didn't know what to think, but I had a sinking feeling that my definition of a good and happy life was about to change.

We prayed together over the phone and that helped relieve a lot of the stress and the worry I could feel building up inside. After our call, I prayed silently on the bus ride home: "Jesus, I don't know what's going on, but what I do know is I need your help to stay strong. Please give me the strength I need, to face whatever lies ahead."

As I stepped off the bus, I pressed 'send' to call my dad. He answered, but as soon as he realized I was not at home yet, he became even more upset. He wouldn't talk to me, saying he had asked me to call him when I was in my room. My anxiety intensified. What on earth was going on?

When I finally reached the privacy of my room, I called my dad again and told him I was alone. His voice seemed different and as soon as he started speaking, I knew instantly it was not good news. As he very quietly explained what had happened, my mind went numb. Through a swirling haze of disbelief I listened as he told me how my mom had killed herself by her own hands. He went on to tell me how sick she had been and how she hadn't been taking her medication anymore, because she didn't think it was necessary to do so.

I could not believe what he was telling me. I got angry. I was upset and very confused. This couldn't be happening! This couldn't be real! Not my mom! Not my mom!

I was curious as to what my brother and sister's reaction was to the news. My dad said he had already talked to them; that they were handling the news about as well as I was taking it. He filled me in on the sketchy funeral plans that had been decided on already with my mom's sister and we agreed to keep each other updated on any discussions and decisions regarding funeral arrangements. Being the oldest sibling, I was a little frightened as to what might be expected of me in the upcoming days. As soon as I felt the anxiety creeping in again, I was reminded of my earlier prayer on the way home, so I took a deep breath and prayed. I asked God to give me strength when, in that moment, I simply wanted to give up.

Prayer will always be the first thing you run to during the entire process of grieving. Even if it is simply, "God, help!" he still hears and will surround you with the comfort and peace you need and more. You need to remember you have a great and powerful God who loves you and will be with you each and every step of the way, helping you to survive and overcome any situation.

*"For I know the plans I have for you," says the Lord. "They are plans for good and not for disaster, to give you a future and a hope. In those days when you pray, I will listen. If you look for me wholeheartedly, you will find me. I will be found by you," says the Lord. "I will end your captivity and restore your fortunes. I will gather you out of the nations where I sent you and will bring you home again to your own land."*

Jeremiah 29:11-14 NLT

# Chapter 2:

---

# TALK TO SOMEONE

*"He comforts us in all our troubles so that we can comfort others. When they are troubled, we will be able to give them the same comfort God has given us."*

2 Corinthians 1:4

It doesn't matter who you talk to, but talk to someone.

When I informed people about the loss of my mom that night, my phone didn't stop ringing. People called to offer their condolences and let me know they were going to be there with me every step of the way. I even remember checking my voicemail and having a new message after clearing the few phone calls already missed. One of my friends, who lived about twenty minutes away, called me to ask if I wanted to come over and spend the night with her so I wouldn't have to be alone. It was such a simple gesture, but it was so very thoughtful and so highly appreciated. In situations such as these, you come to realize that it is the people you know and who you are close to that you need to keep in your life.

When you talk to someone you know and are comfortable talking to, it offers you the support of knowing there is someone who will be there every step of the way; offering an ear to listen, or a shoulder to cry on. You know there is someone out there you can trust and you know they will help you through every moment – especially those moments when all you really want to do is just give up on everything! Talking to someone helps keep your emotions in check, so you don't completely lose your mind. It gives you an outlet where you can express your feelings and, by doing so, you are able to understand, or at least acknowledge, what is going on. The people you talk to may not have the answers you are looking for. They may not have any answers at all; but just knowing they are there with you on your journey makes such a traumatic experience all that much easier to handle.

When all I wanted to do was give up on life myself, others were there to talk to me and lift me up. They encouraged me and helped keep me from falling into a state of depression and all its traps.

Without the support of such people, I wouldn't have been able to make it through some of the harder moments, nor would I be as strong as I am now. They continually encouraged me and gave me the strength I needed. They were being exactly what they were called to be, the hands and feet of Jesus. They extended a hand to help me up when I was falling and they were a strong support when I didn't feel I could take that next step.

*"To everyone who's lost someone they love, long before it was their time. You feel like the days you had were not enough, when you said goodbye."*

Third Day - Cry Out to Jesus

14

# Chapter 3:

## CONSIDER THE OTHERS

It wasn't just my world that was affected: my immediate family, including my two siblings, my dad and my aunts and uncles were all left shaken and grief-stricken about the death of my mom.

In order to get to the funeral, my one brother and I, along with our partners at that time, travelled together. I hadn't seen my brother in quite a few years; I had sincerely anticipated our reunion occurring under better circumstances than what was presented. However, because it took close to twenty-six hours to get to our destination, we were able to catch up on life and what we had been doing since we last saw each other.

By the time we arrived, we were so tired we didn't want to think about the upcoming plans we were going to be faced with the following morning.

Our mom's sister was the last one to have seen our mother alive. Mom had given her sister a note while they were out for lunch and had told her not to open it until after she was gone. Our aunt had no idea what this meant, until after the bill was paid and mom had left. When I asked my aunt if she still had the note, she sadly passed it over to me and my brother; then left the room to give us some privacy to read it.

The note was written in mom's own shaky handwriting, making it hard to read. Her last words spoke of how she loved each one of us deeply and how the things that happened when we were growing up were not our fault. It was heart-wrenching to read her final words. But the greatest heartache, for me, was in knowing that I had talked to her less than a week before this all happened. I started wondering what I could have done to prevent such a devastating end. If I could turn back the clock, could I have seen what was going to happen? Could I have somehow stopped her? Given the circumstances, I wondered, too, how our aunt must be feeling.

When you get a chance to spend time with the people that were also closely affected by the loss, you realize it isn't just your world collapsing; it is your friends' and family's world, too. To know that others were feeling the same grief and sensing the same guilt, did nothing to lessen the pain, but there was solace in the fact that we shared those same emotions.

My advice to you is to keep friends close, but keep those that are affected even closer, because there will always be stories hidden behind what happened; there will be that common thread you all share; there will be collective emotions you can express openly together. You won't know these aspects, if you don't spend time with those closest to the deceased. Consider the others. It might just be that you have something to offer them.

*"Share each other's burdens and in this way obey the law of Christ."*

Galatians 6:2

# Chapter 4:

---

# FIND A SUPPORT SYSTEM

My support system consists of pastors in my local church and close friends I consider to be family. These are people I confide in and ones I can trust to always be there to offer support and a listening ear.

The very first Mother's Day after my mom's suicide was extremely difficult for me. I ran out of the church service in tears, because I didn't have my mother to celebrate with anymore. A close friend saw me run out of the service and came running after me to make sure I was okay. She just took me in her arms and held me. I don't know, to this day, if she understands what that simple gesture meant to me at that time, but it meant a lot! I could never thank her enough for showing me, in that moment, her unconditional love and compassion. It gave me hope that no matter what was going on, or what my emotions were like, there was always going to be someone there to support me and encourage me through every hardship.

There were students in the Bible College I was attending, along with a couple of friends, who helped raise money so I could attend my mother's funeral. And when I was away, there were phone calls from the church calling to ask how things were going. They just wanted to let me know I mattered and they were thinking of me; to tell me they were praying, not only for me, but for my entire family. One of the leaders in the school prayed for me over the phone for everything to go smoothly at the funeral and for a safe journey home when it was all over.

These same people stood by me in prayer the entire time I was dealing with the emotions and the pain of losing my mom. I had people tell me they were surprised to see me still serving and attending church on a weekly basis. I don't know how many times I told them I was not about to slip away from one of the very things that brought me so much joy in life and something that kept me so grounded with people who could always encourage me when I needed it. I knew that if I stopped going, I wasn't going to find the healing and happiness I really needed in my life. It would be too easy to make excuses to stop going altogether if I allowed myself to stop going even once.

I did not want to let life slip away and start getting depressed. I feel that if I had, I would have lost sight of the true destination of what God offered at the end of the journey. If I had not put my trust in God, I would never know how strong I would grow to be. God wants us to trust and obey Him even though our world seems out of control.

I had no idea I was going to come through it as well as I did, but I am so happy I stuck to what I knew to be the right thing, even when it did not feel right. Otherwise, I would not be here right now telling you my story.

Another source of support I found helpful in my darkest times, was the mental health clinic in my area. I went there and talked with a counsellor, just to get my emotions and thoughts out and for some kind of support. In talking with the counsellor, she referred me to a couple of different support groups that met during the week and told me they might help. I went to a few of the meetings and they did help a little bit, but I still found that sticking around the people who mattered the most to me was, ultimately, my greatest source of support and comfort. They were the ones who noticed when I was having a rough time. Even if I just told them what I was feeling, they were there to encourage me; they listened and they cared.

I always thought this tragic death in our family would bring the rest of us a little bit closer, but it didn't change much at all. In fact, when I called my dad on the first anniversary of mom's death to talk about how much I still missed her, my dad told me everyone had moved on with life; that it was about time I did, too. Talk about painful words! I understand my parents had been divorced for quite a few years prior to this, but this was not the type of response I was expecting from my dad at all. I felt a sense of betrayal and injustice that my mother's memory was so easily cast off.

Lately, my dad and I have started talking again. But I do not talk about my mom and he doesn't offer up anything on the subject, either.

What I came to realize over the course of time, is that it is all about who you are close to, who your support system is and who you can trust to call when you need someone to talk to. I wasn't ready to move on at the time and I think, for some people, they never really do feel like moving on after something like this happens. But, at some point, you do need to accept the circumstances and keep moving forward. Even I had to come to terms with that! I found this to be a very difficult part of the process; almost like I was dishonoring my mother by carrying on with life. I did not really want to, but knew it was necessary for my own self-preservation.

Through this process, though, you can still keep the memory of your loved one alive. There are always going to be times when you will want to share an event, or a story about them, with someone. It is at those times that you find out where your support truly comes from.

I was very fortunate to have become close with a couple I consider, now, to be my spiritual mom and dad. I was able to talk to them very openly about what I was feeling and what I was experiencing. They are still always there with a hug, or a smile, that immediately brightens my day. I feel inspired knowing they are always going to be there when I need them.

A family of a very close friend also took me under their wing. I had always called this friend my sister, because we look so much alike and could have passed as siblings. Her parents now call me their daughter and care about me, just as they care for her. The neatest part of it all was when I found out my friend's mom's name was Kathleen, same as my mom; I knew then that this new relationship was God-sent and that I was to honor it and appreciate it.

I want to encourage you that if God plants you somewhere before any traumatic event occurs in your life, stay there. He planted me in a church with lots of support; more than I could ever have expected. There are people all around you that want to encourage you and just tell you that you can make it. Your support system doesn't necessarily have to be comprised of the same people that you are going through the ordeal with. I wasn't close to my family before my mother's death, so I wasn't about to share what I felt with them. I went to those that I had grown close to in my own circles to get the strength and the encouragement I needed.

*"My faith is in a Risen Saviour. My hope's in the One who lives. My faith is trusting in His promise. My life is in His hands."*

Jachin Mullen - Faith Is

# Chapter 5:

---

# HONOR YOUR GRIEF

When you lose someone you love, it is so easy to get depressed and want to give up on yourself; to abandon your dreams and withdraw from life. Ask anyone who has lost a loved one and they will tell you it is one of the most difficult times they have ever had to face.

People constantly told me it would get easier and, eventually, it does. But in those moments where you just want to give up, the reassurance doesn't help you very much. There will be moments when all you want to do is cry. This is a totally natural response to any form of grief. In order to heal, to reach a place of resolution and acceptance, to move on, you have to cry.

One thing that really helped me deal with the shock of my mom being gone, was the peace I felt in knowing she was safely back in God's hands. I had been praying for my mom for about a year before her death. One evening she called me and asked if I was busy. I remember the conversation so clearly - I told her I had a friend over to watch a movie, but certainly had time to talk. She went on to tell me how she had been invited to a barbeque and worship night at a church, where the hospital chaplain pastored. It was there, during prayer, that she had accepted Christ as her personal Lord and Savior. Her voice was still quavering when she described how she had been up dancing before God when, only hours before, she had lots of physical and mental hurts and sores. This was super exciting news for me and I cried with her over the phone. I went to church the next morning, on cloud nine, delighted to share my mom's happiness and elation with all my church family. When I think back to her phone call of good news that night, the tears of happiness I shed often exceed the tears that fall, now that she is gone.

The important thing I had to constantly remind myself was that I needed to grieve and no one was able to do it for me. If it meant breaking down and crying at work, at church, or on my way home from somewhere, I allowed it.

When things got really rough for me, especially in the beginning, I stuck really close to the people who cared about me. I found encouragement in a simple hug, a five-minute conversation before a church service, or just going out for coffee with people I trusted to talk about what I was doing and how I was feeling. I knew that there were people who supported me, cared about me and wanted to know how I was coping with everything. I knew there were people around me that wanted me to come out of it stronger and more resilient. I stopped hanging around people that were negative; ones who were not being supportive in my life. I also filled my life with music that carried powerful, upbeat messages, so I could stay positive and avoid falling back into the abyss of my negative outlook on life and on the world.

In the process of trying to make sense of what happened with your loved one, you may have thoughts of committing the act of suicide yourself. It is a contradictory thought, but it happens to some; I know it happened for me. I thought I was alone in the world with these thoughts, because suicide is pretty much a taboo topic in every-day conversation. There were times I thought there was no one I could be totally honest with. Even if I just wanted to vent, it was difficult not to think the conversation was just being regarded as an attention-seeking ruse.

When you get in this thought pattern, it is very easy to get trapped there. This is where you really need to allow others to help, so they can hold you accountable to your thoughts and make sure you are doing okay. They will let you know if you are off track and help you refocus your life and your thought patterns.

If you, or someone you know, is wanting to, or even starts talking about committing suicide, you need to ask a few hard questions. First, do you have a plan? How are you going to do it? Where? Secondly, do you have the means and the tools to do it? Thirdly, how urgent is it to you? Do you think you are that worthless, that nobody cares; or do you actually have people around you that care that you are just not reaching out to?

For me, I didn't have a plan. I had no idea how to even go about killing myself. I did think that I was worthless, but my problem was that I was not reaching out to the people who did care about me.

Although support groups are great, I found it easiest to open up the hurt and talk to people I already knew. You want to find a path through this dark valley and walk into the light, so find people that will encourage you; ones that you are comfortable talking with. When you need help, you have to ask for it. Otherwise, people do not know how much you really depend on their support.

*"Sometimes my heart is on the ground, and hope is nowhere to be found; love is a figment I once knew and yet I hold on to what I know is true."*

Shawn McDonald - Rise

# Chapter 6:

---

# SAY GOODBYE

The funeral is such a hard thing to get through. It marks your last and only way to really say goodbye to your loved one. When you first hear the news that your loved one is gone, it doesn't seem real. As you go through the motions of planning the funeral, the reality of the situation starts to set in, but when the funeral takes place, that is where the full impact of it all comes crashing down around you. That is when you are jolted awake, realizing that you have to accept things for the way they are.

There are so many critical things to consider when planning a funeral, that it is hard to rank them in any order of importance. You have to decide who is going to speak of the bereavement on your, or the family's, behalf.

Is it going to be another family friend, or a pastor at your church that knew the deceased? Where are you going to hold the funeral? Are you going to have an open or closed casket service, or are you going to have your loved ones' cremated remains in an urn? How many people are you going to have? How many people knew him or her?

My mom was in Cadets for many years before she passed away, so we held the funeral at the base. My boyfriend at the time played the bagpipes, so he piped my brother, sister and I, as well as my mom's siblings in to the service, playing Amazing Grace. The lyrics of the song tore at my heartstrings that day. It really brought the tears to my eyes, knowing that the words were true; that my mom truly did find 'Amazing Grace' and that, now, she was completely free. The lyrics can still bring tears to my eyes and I still hurt a little when I let myself think back to that day.

I really didn't want to face all the people who attended the service. I didn't want to accept the fact that she was gone. I wanted to turn around and leave, but I knew I needed to stay. I knew that I had to have that chance to say goodbye to someone who mattered so much to me.

When you have the funeral for your loved one, go! It is going to be painful and it is going to be hard, but it really is something that you need to do. You need that chance to say goodbye and to be able to add closure to the whole event.

*"Pain is inevitable. It is a part of life. Letting it become a tragedy is a choice."*

Barb Johnston

# Chapter 7:

---

# KEEP A JOURNAL

*"The days when I really need a hug, I have to settle for a friend. All I want is a good mother-daughter hug, mom… and you aren't there."*

Jennifer Boutilier

This is something I wrote in my journal to my mom. Journaling was, and still is, a catharsis for me. It is a medium where I can talk about what is going on; where I can just ramble and let my thoughts and feelings out. It helps me release a lot of pain and emotion when I don't think anyone else will really care. Through writing, I can clearly express what I am feeling, when it becomes too hard to explain to someone else.

There is one particular song I constantly listen to called, *"The Words I Would Say,"* by the Sidewalk Prophets and it talks about the words you wish you could say to someone. This helped me a lot. It made me think of the words I would say to my mother if I still had a chance. One question I asked 'her' quite frequently was, "Why?" I wanted to know why she had committed suicide and I wanted to know why she hadn't talked to someone about her feelings and emotions?

I have a notebook I started using to write letters to my mom. I told my 'notebook mom' things I would have normally called and talked to my mom about - the night I had my first kiss and couldn't stop smiling and, then, when he broke my heart; or when I took on my own Brownie unit, or received a promotion at work. Usually, I write until I can't write anymore, either because I am too tired, or because I have written everything I felt I needed to express. Sometimes, tears start falling and I let them. It is the most relieving feeling, especially after a hard day.

The greatest piece of advice I can give you is to find yourself a notebook you can use to write letters to the person you lost. You might even want to splurge just a little bit and get yourself a really fancy notebook from a stationery store where you can draw and write; somewhere where you can let the tears fall. Having those tear stains on the paper add meaning to the words. It brings out a character inside you where you can look back on the moments and you can remember what you were feeling and why you were feeling that way.

I consider journal writing to be a big part of healing. Not only do you have an outlet where you can acknowledge your pain, but you have a safe, private place to process it without letting it rule your life. The truth is, if you hold onto the pain, chances are you will succumb to it and you lose the opportunity to grow stronger and move forward in your life. You need to let it out, instead of allowing it to boil and fester inside.

*"It's three in the morning and I'm still awake, so I picked up a pen and a page. and I started writing just what I'd say if we were face to face."*

Sidewalk Prophets – Words I Would Say

# Chapter 8:

---

# CRY A LITTLE

People told me many times that it was okay to cry. Even though I knew it was okay and normal to do so, I always felt it inappropriate to do in public settings because, for me, crying is something you do alone.

Since I am the oldest of my siblings, I always felt my feelings were not important. This made the ability to cry difficult. I had always thought that suppressing my feelings was the most appropriate response; that it was more mature to suck it up and stay strong, than to break down and show how weak and frail I was. Even the thought of crying made me feel vulnerable to my surroundings and to my own emotions. Eventually, though, I realized it was the best way for me to deal with the tragic event and to accept what had happened. I finally had to let myself break down those walls I built up and allow myself to cry while going through this process of surviving the aftermath of suicide.

Although there are many people, like me, that do not like to cry, research has shown that crying is actually very good for you. Benefits of crying include reduced stress levels, lowered blood pressure, as well as removal of toxins from your body.

My absolute favorite benefit is that it shows that you are human, which we all are. So, it is perfectly normal to cry. I found a statistic that 85% of women and 73% of men felt less sad and angry after they have had a good cry, which just goes to show that it is detrimental to our health to let emotions and pain stay bottled up inside. We are all human, so if you need a good cry, just allow it to happen – no matter where you are. I have been learning this lesson big time. Besides, having someone embrace you in a hug, makes you realize and remember you are not alone.

When you have lost someone special to you, then the feelings you are experiencing need to be released. Being able to cry always makes you feel better. Crying helps in healing your wounds.

I will be the first to admit that I am not the most beautiful person when I cry. My face turns red, my nose starts running and I am a giant blubbering mess; but after I have had a chance to vent, to let myself cry and just be alone for a bit, I feel better and can go on with life.

I did some research on the power of tears and the most important thing I learned is that tears are 98% water. Keeping your emotions bottled inside actually stresses you out more and that leads to depression. So, you need to cry; you have to cry and it is okay when you do!

*"Crying is not only a human response to sorrow and frustration, it's a healthy one. Crying is a natural way to reduce emotional stress that left unchecked has negative*

*physical effects on the body including the increased risk of cardiovascular disease and other stress related disorders."*

Dr. William H. Frey II. PhD

During the grieving process, you need to let it out. It makes your life easier and it helps others be able to relate to you and you to them.

*"Those who don't know how to weep with their whole heart don't know how to laugh either."*

Golda Meir – Interview in Ms. Magazine (1973)

# Chapter 9:

## BE ANGRY – FOR A LITTLE

## WHILE

*"Don't let the sun go down on your anger; lest you give the devil a foothold"*

Ephesians 4:26

Charles Speilberger (Ph.D.) defines anger as an *"emotional state that can vary in its intensity from a mild irritation to an intense fury and rage"*.
(www.apa.org/topics/anger/control.aspx)

It is a pretty sure bet that any feelings you have during the period of grieving over the loss of your best friend, or family member, may have some form of anger attached to it.

At the time of her death, my mom and I were provinces apart. We had been estranged for many years while I was growing up. When I was nine years old, she had left us and, as the oldest of my siblings, I had to figure out how to deal with this new change of family. I harbored a lot of resentment about her leaving. I always expected that she would come back and be a part of the family again. When she never did, I thought it was because she didn't love us anymore. I thought it was something we had done. In turn, I taught myself to shut down from people for fear of being hurt again.

For many years, I had difficulty building relationships with others, until I realized how lonely my world felt with just me in it. It scared me to think what would transpire if something tragic happened and I had no one around to count on. It was then, that I understood that it was up to me to open up and allow other people into my world.

About three years before her death, my mom and I had even started to rebuild our relationship. It was getting stronger. I felt as though this growing relationship was becoming the kind of connection a mother and daughter would normally have. So, there was a lot of anger and resentment that surfaced when that association was completely and permanently severed.

Being angry is natural and perfectly acceptable, but don't let it stay inside of you and not have a way to release it. You need to be able to talk to people about how you are feeling and to realize it is okay to cry. You have to get to the place of understanding that there wasn't much you could have done to change the situation; committing suicide is usually a last resort; your loved one saw it as the only way out of whatever situation they were in (financial, stress, work, etc.).

According to Speilberger, there are three main approaches to handling anger; expressing, suppressing and calming.

Expressing is the first one I want to talk about, as it is the healthiest way, and the route I finally chose to take. I talked to the people of my church as to who would be a good mentor and a good sounding board as to how I was feeling. I asked around to a few different people and they all gave me the name of the same reference person who, coincidentally, happened to be someone I already knew and had been friends with for a couple years already.

When talking to someone, especially when it comes to venting anger, it helps to be very clear about what your needs are. Be assertive, without being too pushy, or aggressive. Be respectful of the person's time and of their feelings as well. You want to have your needs met; you want to have a healthy outlet for the expression of your anger, but understand they also have needs and feelings.

Having a sounding board was very helpful for me. It gave me a way to express my thoughts to people who I knew would care and listen. Their words were always full of Jesus and His ways, and I knew they truly cared. They pointed me back to the cross and let me know my life had purpose and meaning.

The second way to express your anger is suppressing it. There are times to be angry and express it, but sometimes, it is all about taking control of your anger, stopping the thoughts about whatever is making you angry and focussing on something more positive. The dangerous thing about this step is if your anger doesn't have a way to express itself outward, it turns inward on yourself and can cause hypertension, or depression.

I had personal confirmation of that; when I was going through the grieving process, I turned inward a lot. I felt I was the only one feeling this anger and frustration. I knew I wasn't, but I didn't really know how to allow myself to be open to others, or how to ask for help. I thought I couldn't talk to anyone, relate to anyone, or have anyone relate to me. I went into a very dark space for some time until I could start expressing, outwardly, what I was feeling.

The last approach to dealing with anger is calming down. I used many different strategies to calm myself down. To this day, I still use most of them. Some of my main practices included listening to music, prayer, writing in my journal, or writing a letter to my mom. I also identified greatly with the 'time out' approach, because I would have days where all I wanted to do was cry and shut myself in my room, until I felt human and could be around others. I found I needed to be quiet for a few minutes and allow myself to calm down, journal and/or read, until I felt like I could be human and around people again without bursting into tears. One other important strategy that I relied on was just talking to people. Knowing I wasn't allowed to be shy, was especially important and crucial to my sanity.

Dissipating your anger, in whatever means necessary, doesn't just help your outward behavior toward others, but also your internal responses. It helps lower your heart rate, relaxes your mind and lets your feelings subside. When none of your proven strategies work, that is when, inevitably, someone gets hurt. If you don't do something with your anger, you can develop either an 'I don't care' attitude of apathy, an aggressive behavior, or a personality that is completely unlike who you used to be, or who you want to be. This restricts forward movement because it negatively impacts your relationships with everyone around you, as well as your own state of mind and your healing process.

It would be nice if we could eliminate anger from our vocabulary altogether, but that is just not very realistic. What is important is how you manage the anger you feel. There will be many times where something causes you to be angry. Sometimes it is justifiable; other times, maybe not so much. Fact is, you can't always change the situation, but you can definitely change the way that you react to it. You can choose how you allow it to affect your life.

Being able to handle situations that are difficult can keep you from being unhappy later in life. Even admitting you need help gives you the opportunity to ask those around you for their experience, or knowledge, in an area similar to yours.

*"Don't hold to anger, hurt, or pain. They steal your energy, and keep you from love."*

Leo Buscaglia

# Chapter 10:

## CARRY ON - AS BEST YOU CAN

Even years after your loved one's death, there are memories that are made and you won't be able to share them; Christmas, Easter, birthdays, anniversaries and children being born. The first of these are always the hardest. The very first Christmas where I wanted to call my mom and wish her Merry Christmas and ask her how things were going, I had to remind myself I couldn't do that.

The next summer, my best friend got married. It wasn't until the reception that evening, that I realized my mom wasn't going to see me walk down the aisle to meet my new husband. This brought a new wave of tears, just wanting to have my mom back.

The date I found the hardest was the anniversary of my mom's death. On that day, I took my mom's ashes and put them in a spot where I love to go; a peaceful spot where I go with friends and family. I try to make it there at least a few times during the year just to be alone for a couple hours and spend time with my mom and to allow myself some time to grieve, even when it's most painful. It gives me time to reflect on the year, on things I would say to her and what I have done and what has been going on in my life. I make sure to bring my notebook and just write and pray.

As a young adult, I searched for someone who I could look up to; someone who I could call my mother, so I could still have those mother-daughter conversations that I knew I needed to have every once in a while. I found the 'notebook mom' to be a very important tool in my life, but having the 'surrogate mom' I was blessed to get to know, provided me a way to actually talk to someone who I could trust about how I felt and what was going on in my life. This couple that 'adopted' me are people who I want, and choose, to be with. They have been positive influences in my life; not about to let me second guess myself, or to allow me to doubt where I was in life. They were ones that, once they heard the news, thought of my well-being first and made sure that I was doing okay.

If they could sense that I was withdrawing, they made me talk until I told them what was actually going on in my life, until it got down to why I was feeling like I did. They helped me to fully analyze my situation and look for solutions, instead of faking the perfect life and hiding the sorrow I was really feeling. These people could see through me. They could tell I needed some support and help. They were there to just listen, offer guidance if needed and point me in a direction that would prove to be beneficial and positive.

Keep close to your friends and family. Don't let yourself get distant. Don't forget who the deceased was to you, or the role they played in your life. And for sure, do not forget about your relationship to others.

I still write in my journal and I still write in my 'letters to mom' notebook, but not as often as I used to when I first started. I have had to come to a place of acceptance that my mom is really gone and there is nothing I can do to bring her back. I have had to go to that peaceful place within and not let the things that hurt before, hurt quite as much. I still visit the place where I am the happiest and where I find the most peace.

*"Praise God we don't have to hide scars. They just strengthen our wounds and soften our hearts. They remind us of where we have been, but not who we are."*

Jonny Diaz - Scars

# Epilogue

As you were reading this, you probably noticed that I refer to God frequently and mention how important it was for me that I stick close to my church and my church family. That mattered to me a lot, simply because it gave me a way to stay grounded in my faith. There is a story in the Bible that says, *"if you build your house on the sand and a storm comes, your house is gone. But if you build your house on the solid rock which is Jesus Christ, you can withstand a storm"*. (Luke 6:46-49 NLT)

Jesus Christ, God's one and only son came down to Earth to live a perfect, sinless life. He died for our sins on a sinner's cross so that we can join him in Heaven when we die. (John 3:16NLT)

If you would like to have this relationship with Jesus, if you understand that you can't live life as you were designed to live and you want to see life with an eternal perspective, then I would like to invite you to pray this prayer with me: "Jesus, I thank you for your life that you lived here on Earth, so that I can join you in Heaven. I understand what you did for me on the cross. I understand that I am a sinner and I ask for your forgiveness and I would like to accept you into my life and take control of my life right now, in Jesus' name. Amen."

If you have honestly prayed this prayer and want to learn more, I would love to hear about it.

**Please email me at:**
jennifer.boutilier@outlook.com;

I would love to help you get connected and help you in the next stages of your life.

# References

Third Day; *Cry Out to Jesus*;
EMI, 2005 – CD

Mullen, Jachin; *Faith Is*;
Red Leaf, 2012 – CD

McDonald, Shawn; *Rise*;
Be music & Entertainment, 2011 – CD

Johnston, Barbara; *Stick a Geranium in Your Hat and Be Happy*; Dallas, Texas, Thomas Nelson, 2004.

Sidewalk Prophets; *Words I Would Say*;
Word Entertainment, 2009 – CD

Frey, William H.; 5 *Reasons Why Crying is Good for You*; Care2 make a difference; June, 2011 - Website

Speilberger, Charles. (Ph.D.); *What is Anger?* American Psychological Association - N.D. Website

Buscaglia, Leo; *GoodReads*; N.P. 2014 - Website.

Diaz, Jonny; *Scars;* 2012 - CD

All scripture verses are quoted from the New Living Translation version.

# About the Author

Jenn Boutilier lives in Red Deer, Alberta, and spends time loving life and loving the world she lives in. She volunteers with Girl Guides of Canada on a weekly basis, teaching young girls how to live strong and follow their dreams. She enjoys sharing her time with friends and with her church family, growing in faith and in relationship to the people that kept her going through the pain and torment of her mother's death. As a survivor of the aftermath of suicide, Jenn hopes that her journey from the dark into the light will give inspiration and hope to others faced with the same crisis in their lives.

If you would like to purchase this book in bulk *or* if you have any questions about distribution, please contact the publisher.

**Aurora Publishing**
Email: aurorapublishing@shaw.ca
PH: 403-230-5946 x 1
www.ABookIsNeverABook.com